Original title:
Pineapple Dreams

Copyright © 2025 Creative Arts Management OÜ
All rights reserved.

Author: Evelyn Hartman
ISBN HARDBACK: 978-1-80586-231-4
ISBN PAPERBACK: 978-1-80586-703-6

## **Vibrant Canopy**

Under the bright, yellow sun,
A crown of green awaits for fun.
Laughter drips from every leaf,
As I dance, with joy, like a thief.

Sipping juice from a funky cup,
I wiggle my toes, I wiggle them up!
A squishy fruit in hand, oh my!
Who knew a plant could make me fly!

## **Sun-Drenched Whimsy**

In a land where giggles grow,
Limes are jealous of the show.
A fountain of sweetness, bright and neat,
Is it the fruit, or just my beat?

Sunshine spills like syrupy rain,
As I trip on a root, but I can't complain!
With a snack that brings the skies to play,
I'll skip and hop my goofy way!

## Urban Oasis

Amidst the streets, a fruity glow,
Tropical vibes begin to flow.
Cars honk loud, but I don't care,
My mind's on sunshine, warm and rare.

People start to stop and stare,
At my wobbly, fruity chair.
Bouncing up like a rubber band,
In this city, I'm a fruity stand!

## **Sweetened Memories**

In my dreams, a fruit parade,
With every twist, a new escapade.
Hats made of zest, they dance around,
In this fruity circus, joy is found.

A plushy friend with a greenish crown,
Winks at me, then tumbles down.
We giggle loud, like kids at play,
In this sugary realm, we'll sway all day!

## Nature's Sweet Song

In fields where fruits collide,
The laughter cannot hide.
A crown upon a sphere,
Crafts giggles far and near.

The wind it whispers bold,
With tales of yellow gold.
A dance of zestful cheer,
With laughter ringing clear.

## Ripe Reflections

In a world of fruity rays,
We bask in sunny days.
With a chuckle and a cheer,
Sweet visions seem so near.

A twist of fate we find,
With smiles so unconfined.
Round and ripe, a joyful sight,
We toast to stars at night.

## **Serendipitous Shores**

On sandy paths we roam,
Where every wave feels like home.
A splash of joy on sunlit days,
In fruity and funny ways.

We gather fruits like treasures,
With laughter, oh, such pleasures!
The beachballs bounce and whirl,
As giggles skip and twirl.

## **The Juicy Journey**

With every twist and turn we take,
Adventures made, no rules to break.
A slice of joy, a fruity grin,
Our journey's where the laughs begin.

In every bite, a giggle blooms,
Celebration fills the rooms.
Let's raise a glass and sing aloud,
For silly fun, we're ever proud!

## **Pastel Sunsets**

A fruit in a crown, so bright and so round,
It wears a gold hue, like a sun that's just found.
With shades of soft pink and a dash of delight,
It tickles the taste buds, a joyous bite.

In gardens of laughter, it sways to the beat,
With party hats on, it's the life of the street.
Like candy-coated clouds on a sugar high ride,
The sunset giggles as flavors collide.

## The Dance of Flavor

Oh, twist and twirl, in the bowl you will see,
Fruits doing the limbo, as goofy as can be.
With citrusy tang and a splash of warm cheer,
They cha-cha together, drawing everyone near.

A conga line forms, with giggles and grins,
As watermelon winks, and the mango spins.
Each slice tells a story, a fruit masquerade,
Where laughter is plenty, and worries just fade.

## Tropical Tranquility

In hammocks of laughter, we sway side to side,
A peaceful adventure, our fruity joy ride.
With coconuts clinking and laughter that sings,
The essence of summer in our hearts, it clings.

A tropical whisper, with giggles on shore,
Where mango and banana keep asking for more.
The sun dips below with a wink and a grin,
In this fruitful paradise, the fun will begin.

## **Slices of Adventure**

Cutting through laughter, a knife in the air,
Each slice tells a tale, of whimsy to share.
A juicy explosion, with every bright bite,
In our silly cuisine, the flavors ignite.

We backpack through kitchens, explore every jar,
With giggles and splashes, we shine like a star.
In a world made of fruit, our mischief won't end,
Each adventure we savor, a joke, a good friend.

## **Pirate's Fruit**

A pirate sailed on seas so wide,
In search of treasure, his heart full of pride.
He found a fruit, oh what a sight,
With a crown so tall, it gave him a fright.

He took a bite, expecting a gold,
But instead got juice that was warm and bold.
He laughed so hard, the waves joined in,
For fruity humor was sure to win.

## **Tasteful Adventures**

In a land where flavors play and dance,
A fruit gave all who tried a chance.
With sweetness bright and moods so light,
It turned each meal into pure delight.

A spoonful here, a slice or two,
In bowls and drinks, it wiggled through.
With giggles and grins, a feast was spread,
Adventure began with each vibrant shred.

## **Breezy Escapes**

Under the sun, a beach so bright,
With smooth sands and kites in flight.
A fruit rolled by, oh such a tease,
It whispered tales in the gentle breeze.

It danced on waves, played hide and seek,
Tickling toes and making folks peek.
With laughter loud, it bounced around,
A cheerful spirit, joy unbound.

## Lush Imaginings

In gardens green, where laughter sprang,
A fruit that giggled, and slightly sang.
It wore a jacket, yellow and bright,
A sight so silly, it felt just right.

The sunbeams tickled its rounded shell,
Where stories of fruit and fun would dwell.
It promised a party, each slice a chance,
To turn the mundane into a dance.

## Dances of the Exotic Fruit

In the land where fruits do sway,
A spiky orb decides to play.
With a twist and shimmy, it starts to groove,
The entire orchard begins to move.

Bananas laugh, they swing in glee,
While coconuts roll, wild and free.
Lemons compete with silly twirls,
As the antics unfold, laughter unfurls.

A mango jumps, it shimmies wide,
While the papaya takes a slide.
The harvest moon is here to see,
Fruit fiesta, what a sight to be!

With every pop and every cheer,
The juiciest party of the year.
From sweet to sour, they all unite,
In the dances of the fruit delight.

## Sweet Serenade in the Tropics

Under the sun, so warm and bright,
A fruity tune takes flight at night.
A chorus of berries hums a tune,
While the coconut bops like a cartoon.

Strawberries twirl in polka dots,
Dancing with pineapples in funny slots.
Mangoes sing with a voice so sweet,
As they shuffle to the tropical beat.

Watermelons giggle, rolling about,
While oranges cheer with a happy shout.
In this parade of joy and cheer,
Every fruit is welcome, year after year.

They strum some limes, the mood's just right,
With juicy rhythms that feel just right.
In this serenade, we can't resist,
The laughter of fruits in tropical mist.

## Echoes of Island Joy

On a beach where flavors blend,
The fruit serenade knows no end.
Coconuts clink in a joyful cheer,
Echoing laughter far and near.

Berries bounce in the salty breeze,
While oranges dance with graceful ease.
The laughter rises with every wave,
A fruity party, the island's rave.

Bananas swing from palm to palm,
Unleashing chaos, a fruity charm.
In this echo of jubilant fun,
Even the shadows come out to run.

With every twist, every playful spin,
The fruits unite, a feast to win.
Island joy in every bite,
An echo of laughter, pure delight.

## The Lush Fruit's Secret

In the grove where secrets lie,
A guava whispers, oh so sly.
The mango winks and starts to beam,
Saying, 'Join us in our fruity dream!'

The durian's grin, a funny sight,
While the starfruit shines, oh so bright.
In this lush realm of wacky fun,
The fruit's true secrets have just begun.

A riddle spun by the kiwi glow,
The sweetest tales that nobody knows.
Papaya giggles with a cheeky grin,
As watermelon rolls while joining in.

With every nibble, a laugh is found,
In this fruit kingdom, joy abounds.
The lush fruits dance under the sun,
Revealing secrets, oh what fun!

## **Mosaic of Sunshine**

In fields of yellow, bright and sweet,
A fruit so funny, none can beat.
Wobbling on the table, it stands proud,
Like a jester, making all laugh loud.

With leafy hair and a spiky style,
It charms the room, stays for a while.
A juicy laugh in every bite,
Turning munching into pure delight.

A tropical dance upon the plate,
Reminds us all to celebrate.
With giggles sprouting from every core,
This fruity fun we can't ignore.

## The Golden Twilight

When day meets night, a swirl of cheer,
A fruit slice winks as it draws near.
Golden glow on a summer's eve,
A giggle wrapped, you won't believe!

It rolls and tumbles off the shelf,
Whispering jokes, 'I'm quite myself!'
Dressed in shades of yellow and green,
A playful mood, like none you've seen.

We toast to laughter, sunlit fun,
As fruit and giggles come undone.
Under the sky, the stars all beam,
This fruity wonder fuels our dream.

## Captivating Flora

In gardens where the silly blooms,
A punchline laughs amid the rooms.
Petals yellow, bright as day,
This fruity jest is here to play.

With crowns of green and smiles to spare,
It twirls around without a care.
A quirky friend in summer's glow,
Spreading joy wherever it goes.

In bowls of fruit, it takes the lead,
Delivering laughter, that's guaranteed!
A slice of sunshine, quirky and bold,
Tales of joy in every fold.

## Luminous Whimsy

In kitchens bright, a jester stands,
Chasing giggles, with funny hands.
Winking fruit with stories to share,
In every slice, a joke laid bare.

It bounces high, in playful glee,
Tickling noses, oh what a spree!
With laughter sweet as honeyed rays,
It fills our hearts on sunny days.

From smoothies bright to pies anew,
This whimsical fruit, forever true.
With every bite, comedy's found,
In fruity laughter, joy abound.

## **Tropical Reverie**

In a world of juicy delight,
Where the fruit's wearing shades so bright,
Coconuts giggle on the shore,
Waving to the mango corps.

Hula dancers spin with glee,
Monkeys jump from tree to tree,
The sun's a giant disco ball,
With fruity tunes for one and all.

Waves crash in a rhythmic cheer,
Tropical vibes are always near,
Sipping on a drink so cool,
Laughter echoes, that's the rule.

Every snack is a comedy,
Bananas slip—oh, what a spree!
In this land of zesty play,
Funny fruits lead the way!

## The Golden Slice

Golden wonders on my plate,
This fruity treasure, oh so great,
Laughing as I take a bite,
Sweetness dances—what a sight!

Giggles float upon the breeze,
Fruit salads that aim to please,
With cherries, berries, all combined,
A laughter feast, oh how refined!

The juicy juice spills on my chin,
As I dive into this fruity sin,
Watermelon's a jolly fool,
Making summer feel so cool.

Slices stack, oh what a tower,
While pineapple holds the power,
In this kitchen, fun is rife,
Every taste adds to my life!

## **Beneath the Sunlit Canopy**

Underneath the leafy shade,
Fruity snacks are casually laid,
Berries bounce from tree to vine,
In this place, all tastes align.

Coconut laughs, it breaks the shell,
Jokes are shared, oh can you tell?
Oranges roll like little clowns,
Spreading joy all through the towns.

Sunlight beams, a golden glow,
While sticky fingers steal the show,
Every bite brings out a cheer,
Here's to jests and fruity beer!

Piña coladas in our cups,
Even grapes are making ups,
Beneath this vast and vibrant sky,
Life's a party, oh my, my!

## **Juicy Whispers of Paradise**

Whispers drift from vibrant trees,
Fruits in chorus with the breeze,
Tropical accents, oh so sweet,
In paradise, we dance on feet.

Limes are laughing, lemons flirt,
Dancing with their floral skirt,
Every flavor, a chuckling face,
In this zany fruit-filled space.

Grapefruit's on a funny spree,
Poking fun at you and me,
Jokes as sour as its taste,
But in this land, there's no such waste.

As night falls, the laughter glows,
With every dark, a fruit still shows,
A festival of light and cheer,
In juicy whispers, we revere!

## Golden Tropic Bliss

In a land where sun does gleam,
Coconuts dance, a funny dream.
Laughter floats on salty air,
Silly hats upon heads, we wear.

Tropical drinks with crazy straws,
Belly laughs break all the laws.
In this bliss, we jump and roll,
Life's a party—let's lose control.

## **Reflections on Sandy Shores**

Footprints leading to nowhere fast,
Crabs in chorus, a silly cast.
Waves tickle toes, a splashy game,
Seagulls squawk, but who's to blame?

Hats blown away, they soar like kites,
Chasing sunbeams through wild fights.
We giggle as we chase the tide,
Matching laughter, we can't hide.

**Tropical Whispers**

Coconut shells make perfect drums,
Watch us dance, oh here it comes!
A parrot jokes with witty flair,
Wiggly toes in the salty air.

Bamboo huts with quirky signs,
Even our shadows crack funny lines.
In this realm of sun and cheer,
Every moment brings a sneer!

## **Sunlit Serenade**

Banana boats that zip and zoom,
In a world that's full of bloom.
Sunglasses perched on goofy glares,
Counting clouds like wild bears.

Salsa moves on the beach so fine,
Flip-flops flying, crossing the line.
With giggles echoing through the breeze,
Here's to joy, we dance with ease!

## Whimsical Delight

Beneath the sun, they twirl and dance,
With leaves so green, they love to prance.
In tropical shores, they wear a crown,
Their prickly skin, a funny frown.

They giggle sweetly, drop like rain,
In punchy drinks or on a train.
A splash of color, a burst of glee,
In a fruit salad, oh, what a spree!

The beach ball bounces, oh what a sight,
With yellow streaks that are pure delight.
They dream of parties with bubbly cheer,
Where laughter bursts, and friends draw near.

So here we stand, fruits on our head,
With goofy grins, enough said!
In a world where joy takes the lead,
These quirky guys plant a funny seed.

## Treasures of the Tropics

In the tropics, secrets hide,
Beneath the sun, they stand with pride.
A treasure chest, oh what a sight,
With golden jewels, pure delight!

They giggle softly as they grow,
In the wind's soft dance, they sway and flow.
With spiky tops like hair so wild,
Each fruity grin, a quirky child.

The nectar flows, a sweet surprise,
With every bite, joy brightly flies.
In smoothies thick, or by the slice,
Tropical treasures, oh how nice!

On sandy shores, they roll about,
With silly hats and joyful shout.
A feast of laughter under the sun,
These fruity gems are always fun!

## Golden Dreams in a Hollow

In a hollow heart, gold dreams reside,
With sunshine sparkles in every ride.
Quirky shapes and silly sounds,
In this fruity world, laughter abounds.

They bounce like balls, so round and bright,
In cozy nooks, what a funny sight!
With juice that flows in rivers sweet,
A joyful dance, we can't be beat!

In the hollow, friends gather near,
With quirky tales that bring good cheer.
Each slice reveals a giggly twist,
In this paradise, joy can't be missed.

With every bite, the silliness swells,
As laughter rings like joyful bells.
Golden dreams in a fruity place,
Where joy and fun fill every space!

## **A Taste of Paradise**

In paradise, a splash of fun,
With flavors bright, oh what a run!
Each golden fruit with a quirky grin,
A dance of joy that pulls us in.

Like sunshine in a wobbly cup,
They giggle lightly, we can't get enough.
Each juicy bite, a burst of cheer,
In this fruity world, we persevere.

Tropical nights, a silly parade,
With fruits that wear their crowns, they wade.
A taste of laughter, a twist of fate,
In every slice, joy won't wait!

So raise a toast to the fun we share,
With fruity delights floating in the air.
In this paradise where laughter streams,
We savor life and all its dreams.

# Radiance in a Pinwheel

A fruit so bright, it spins with glee,
Wearing a crown, it's sweet as can be.
With laughter bubbling like a sunny brew,
Come take a ride in this fruity zoo.

Laughter erupts at the carnival stand,
A juggling act with a fruity hand.
It dances around with a zesty grin,
Who knew a fruit could be such a win?

Jokes fly high on this merry-go-round,
With lemony friends all laughing around.
Let's toast with slices, put your hands up too,
In the fruity world, there's fun to pursue!

## Silhouette of a Tropical Eden

Under the sun, where giggles play,
A golden slice brightens the day.
Palm trees sway with a shimmy and shake,
Whispering secrets to the fruitcake.

In tropical hues, we prance and roam,
These sugary dreams feel like home.
With waves of laughter and tangy delight,
Feasting all day, from morning to night.

Bouncing around in a fruity parade,
Serenading the sun with a sweet charade.
As chocolate rivers flow with flair,
Who knew paradise could be so rare?

## **A Sip of Sunshine**

A shake in hand, a smile so wide,
Sipping the sun, oh what a ride!
With cherries on top and a tease of lime,
This drink's a reason to dance in rhyme.

Frothy laughter spills with each gulp,
Bouncing flavors cause a happy yelp.
With minty breezes in this drink parade,
Each sip adds joy, like a lively charade.

Riding the waves of citrus delight,
Every drink is a party, oh what a sight!
So join the fun, it's time to unwind,
In this frothy bliss, happiness we find!

## **The Enchanted Orchard**

In a grove where laughter sings,
Fruits wear crowns, like golden kings.
Twirls and giggles flutter about,
In this magical place, there's no room for doubt.

Tickling trees that sway and giggle,
Our funny peels make the best riddle.
Each bite a smile, juicy and sweet,
Exploring this wonder feels like a treat.

Here fruits wear shoes, ready to dance,
Join the bash, don't miss your chance!
With every rumble of silly delight,
This enchanted orchard feels just right!

## Essence of the Exotic

In a Land of Yellow Whirl,
Where spiky crowns twirl.
They dance in sunny cheer,
With laughter in the air.

Wobbling on the plate,
Oh, what a funny fate!
Sipping juice so sweet,
My taste buds skip a beat.

With funny hats they wear,
A feast that's quite rare.
Sticky fingers, don't you mind?
In this fruit, joy you will find!

As I try to take a bite,
It rolls up to take flight!
Catching it is quite the game,
But oh, it's worth the fame!

## Sunkissed Daydream

Under the bright sun's ray,
A fruit just wants to play.
Shining bright and oh so sweet,
Dreams of summer can't be beat.

Chasing down this juicy treat,
While dodging the ants' compete.
Giggles burst with every squeeze,
As juice flows like a breeze.

Turning corners on the floor,
Slipping, sliding, wanting more!
Twirling like a merry song,
In this dream, nothing's wrong.

Laughter bubbles, smiles galore,
As juicy tumbles I adore.
Who knew happiness could drip,
From a silly fruity lip?

## Bubbling Bliss

In a bowl so bright and round,
Happiness can be found.
Sipping potion from the rim,
Life feels sweeter, on a whim.

Bubbles rise, they pop and play,
Bringing sunshine to the day.
Giggles as the flavor sings,
Joyful chaos laughter brings.

With a wave of frothy foam,
This tasty drink feels like home.
Tickling taste buds in delight,
What a wondrous, silly sight!

Floating fruit and silly hops,
Bubbling bliss never stops.
As I dance around the room,
The fruity joy begins to bloom.

## **Orchard of Serenity**

In a garden filled with cheer,
Fruits are bouncing, oh so near.
Smiles hang from every vine,
Nature's laughter so divine.

Swinging from a leafy tree,
A fruity friend swings with glee.
Bouncing like it's full of jokes,
Even all the laughing folks!

Whispering breezes gently sway,
As juicy giggles find their way.
With every crunch, a burst of fun,
In this calm where laughter's spun.

Giggling leaves, the sun aglow,
Who knew fruits could steal the show?
In this orchard's merry stream,
Life's a joyful, silly dream!

## Fragrant Futures

In a land where fruits do giggle,
Where juiciness makes everyone wiggle.
A crown of gold upon a head,
Whispers of style, it surely said.

Sipping smoothies from a cup,
With flavors that make the world erupt.
Tropical tales in every bite,
A dance of joy, oh what a sight!

Bananas blush, coconuts clink,
While citrus fruits join in to wink.
In this mix of silly fun,
Beneath the bright and shining sun.

So let us toast with fruity cheer,
To quirky cravings far and near.
In baskets brimming full of delight,
Each slice a giggle, pure and bright!

## **Enchanted Bounties**

In orchard shade, a twist awaits,
Where nature plays creative states.
A jester's hat, a melon's grin,
Each fruit's a laugh, let's dive right in.

Mangoes sway in breezy jest,
Avocados give their very best.
With every bite, a chuckle flows,
As grapes roll by on tiny toes.

The citrus burst, a zesty cheer,
Kiwis dance, oh my, so dear!
With fruit salads piling up high,
Tickling noses, oh me, oh my!

Let's gather round, don't be shy,
With fruity giggles, we'll fly high.
Each morsel, a riddle, wrapped in zest,
In this enchanted feast, we're all guests!

## **Luminous Abundance**

Golden suns on tropical shores,
Fruit stands filled with silly wars.
Where apples wear polka dot hats,
And pears perform in dance with bats.

Watermelon smiles wide and bright,
Sparkling juices, sheer delight.
Bananas giggle, slipping down,
As cherries wear their rosy crown.

A tangerine's wily disguise,
Makes everyone smile and surprise.
Carambola, the starry treat,
Turns each moment into a feat.

So let's celebrate this fruity spree,
From the orchard to jubilee.
Each slice a comedy divine,
In this luminous world, we shine!

## Serene Gusts

In the garden where laughter grows,
Fruits like stories, in rows they pose.
Peaches gossip with sweet delight,
Beneath the trees, the world feels right.

Breezes tickle bananas and limes,
Ticking like clocks, oh, how they chime!
Kiwi jokes that make you clap,
Each bite has a funny trap.

With cups of juice, we toast and cheer,
To fruity fun that draws us near.
In this serene, whimsical space,
Joyful faces fill the place.

The laughter echoes in the sun,
As we munch and joke, oh what fun!
With every fruit, a happy scene,
In gusts of joy, we live the dream!

## Bountiful Harmony

In a tropic land, so bright and fair,
Laughter dances in warm, sweet air.
Fruit hats are worn, a comical sight,
Sipping juice, as day turns to night.

Coconuts roll, on sandy shores,
Playful waves call, nature's roars.
Juggling melons, a circus at noon,
Dance with shadows, hum a funny tune.

Crab in a tux, with a tiny bowtie,
Winks at the seagulls flying high.
Sunsets drip gold into the sea,
Every giggle feels wild and free.

Life's a feast, with flavors galore,
Tickling taste buds, and spirits soar.
Bananas fly, on the breeze they glide,
In this cheerful realm, we take a ride.

## The Scent of Summer


Whiffs of citrus, float through the air,
Funny little critters dance without care.
Fragrance of fruit that makes you grin,
Every sunny day feels like a win.

Rainbows hide in a splash of juice,
Laughing still, no excuse to refuse.
Mangoes giggle, as they tumble down,
Bouncing off cheeks, this fruity crown.

Garden gnomes, in a fruit parade,
With jelly beans, their worries fade.
Sprinkle of giggles on buttercream skies,
Sunshine giggles, 'what a surprise!'

Cupcakes on clouds, a whimsical sight,
Every sprinkle holds pure delight.
Join the laughter, taste the splendor,
In the fruit dance, we're all the contenders.

## Waves of Euphoria

Tidal waves crash, giggles explode,
Surfing the silliness, down this road.
Coconuts bob, in a wacky race,
Ocean's tickle, they keep their pace.

Jellyfish twirl, with hats askew,
Cartwheeling fish, blow bubbles too.
Clouds of whipped cream float overhead,
In this frothy world, no one feels dread.

Shells whisper secrets, all under the sun,
Jokes exchanged, just having fun.
Tanning sunflowers, in colorful bloom,
Each petal's a smile, lighting the room.

Life's a carnival, laughter our game,
In this paradise, nothing's the same.
Ride the waves on a giggly spree,
In this joyous chaos, we're wild and free.

## The Honeyed Horizon

Golden sunsets, drape the sky,
Buzzy creatures hum, oh my oh my!
Lollipop trees in the soft, warm glow,
Each swaying branch shares tales of woe.

Silly shadows play peek-a-boo,
Tickled by breezes, fresh and new.
Waltzing flowers, with petals so bright,
A parade of colors, pure delight.

Honey drips slow from the bees' dance,
Life's a treat, put on your pants!
Swinging on branches, cheerfully steep,
Under this magic, there's no time for sleep.

Radiant laughter, echoes afar,
Join the fun, 'neath the evening star.
In this delight, we twirl and sway,
Thankful for sweetness, every day.

## Symphony of Citrus

In the land of fruity songs,
Where the giggles grow so strong,
Lemons dance with their bright cheer,
While oranges roll without fear.

Grapefruit joins the merry band,
Twisting in a citrus stand,
Bananas slip with laughter loud,
Bouncing like a silly crowd.

Beneath the sun's warm glowing beam,
Everyone is part of the scheme,
Melodies of flavors blend,
With fruity friends that never end.

## **Whispering Palms**

The palms sway gently in the breeze,
Sharing tales of fruit-filled trees,
We laugh as coconuts take flight,
And mangoes dance with sheer delight.

A parrot squawks a silly tune,
As pineapples wear a goofy balloon,
With laughter tickling the air,
Tropical humor everywhere.

The sun shines down on this funny lot,
Where every fruit's a perfect shot,
Chasing shadows, playing games,
In this world where joy reclaims.

## **Cluster of Joy**

A group of fruits in joyful throng,
Playing games all night long,
The cherries giggle, round and sweet,
While pears trip over their own feet.

The berries bounce with cheerful grace,
Racing each other in a fun-filled chase,
Kiwi spins and makes a scene,
As laughter echoes where they've been.

In this cluster, smiles abound,
With every joke a silly sound,
A fruity party, never grim,
Where every hour feels like a whim.

## **Warm Embrace of the Tropics**

In the tropics where the sun is bright,
Fruits gather 'round, what a sight!
Pineapples wear their favorite hats,
While coconuts roll like silly cats.

The warmth wraps round like a soft hug,
As limes perform a funny tug,
With every twist and joyful yell,
This fruity fiesta casts a spell.

Group hugs from bananas so sweet,
As they share their grand retreat,
In laughter's arms, we all unite,
Celebrating life, oh what a delight!

## Juicy Fantasies

Under the shade of a giant fruit,
I found a treasure, oh what a hoot!
A crown on top, a prickly delight,
I danced with joy, oh what a sight!

With a twist and a turn, I took a sip,
Of a smoothie made from an ocean trip.
My funny hat wobbled, then flew away,
Chasing it, I laughed all day!

In a world where fruit sings and sways,
I role-played as king in fruity arrays.
Sipping sunshine from my golden cup,
I smiled so big, I could erupt!

Oh, to dream in this juicy land,
Where laughter flows like grains of sand.
Banana boats and coconut views,
I sailed through life, it felt like snooze!

## **Golden Horizon**

From the shore, the sun greets me wide,
Golden hues reflect the ocean's pride.
I wear my shades and a silly grin,
Waves of laughter wash over my chin.

With coconuts hugged in a sandy throne,
I hosted a party, all on my own.
Fruit hats on heads, we twirled and spun,
With each wobbly dance, we had so much fun!

The seagulls squawked in a comical tone,
Trying to steal the fruit I'd grown.
Balancing jokes on the tip of my nose,
I chuckled out loud as the fruit circus grows!

As daylight fades, we stay in this bliss,
Missing the point of what we might miss.
Here's to horizons that never end,
With goofy friends to forever send!

## **Sweet Slices of Hope**

In a fruit bazaar with colors so bright,
I found a slice that brought pure delight.
With every bite, the laughter flows,
It tickled my taste buds, oh how it glows!

Wearing sunglasses, I posed with flair,
Fruits on my head, who would dare?
Lemon launches and cherry bombs,
Crafting sweet tales that bring the qualms.

Under the sun, we crack jokes and cheers,
As melon laughter drowns out our fears.
Watermelon smiles and papaya fests,
In this slice of life, we feel truly blessed!

With every fruit created, joy grows high,
As we giggle and munch beneath the sky.
A hope so sweet, it won't easily fade,
In this fruity world, we've joyously played!

## **Exotic Daydreams**

In a land of fruit, I found my muse,
A dragonfruit dancing in shiny shoes.
With its quirky form and colors so bold,
It told me secrets that were pure gold.

Beneath the palm, I twirled like a fool,
Dancing with coconuts—my very own school.
With each little bop and a wiggly shake,
Even the pineapple joined with a quake!

As I frolicked in peaches and plums,
The giggles echoed, creating big drums.
Happiness sparked in the air like a song,
In this exotic space where I belong.

In the garden of whimsy and laughter galore,
Every bite is a dream, who could want more?
From fruity delights to the stars so bright,
In this daydream, I find pure delight!

## Orchard of Delights

In a field where oddities grow,
Fruits in hats that steal the show,
Lemonade rivers, pickles in boats,
Dancing mangoes wearing funny coats.

Silly strawberries sing in tune,
Under the giggling, bright-faced moon,
The apples chase the bumblebees,
While pears giggle in the gentle breeze.

Radishes wearing roller skates,
Hop about with endless fates,
While cherries chuckle at a joke,
As the broccoli grows, a friendly bloke.

Lemon trees do a silly jig,
While elderberries bust a big,
In this garden of laughter and cheer,
Every fruit dreams without fear.

## **Celestial Fruits**

Stars twinkle upon the fruity night,
Watermelons float with pure delight,
The bananas are dressed in polka dots,
Playing hopscotch in the cosmic plots.

Oranges bounce on fluffy clouds,
Winking down at the silly crowds,
Kiwi clowns juggle radish pies,
While starfruit giggles and gently sighs.

Grapes strum tunes with viney strings,
Whispering secrets of cosmic flings,
Plums in capes fly round the moon,
As apples dream to a jazzy tune.

Tangerine twirls in the dreamy sky,
While raspberries laugh and wave goodbye,
In this celestial, fruity parade,
Joy and laughter shall never fade.

## Caribbean Reverie

On sandy shores where coconuts sway,
Mangoes sunbathe through the day,
Pineapples wearing shades so fine,
Sip coconut milk from a golden shrine.

Tropical fish tap dance with glee,
Under the shade of a tall palm tree,
The beach towels all sing in a row,
While the ocean tickles, pulling toes.

Papayas play maracas in the sun,
With guavas laughing, oh what fun!
Bikini-clad lemons join the spree,
Jumping waves and setting them free.

In this land where the laughter flows,
Every fruit wears a colorful pose,
As the sun and sea join in the game,
Caribbean dreams will never be the same.

## Lush Havens

In a shady grove, where giggles sprout,
Pumpkins grinning with no doubt,
The cherries dance with wicked flair,
Under the blossoms that fill the air.

Nutty buddies play hide and seek,
With jellybeans wiggling on a streak,
The cucumbers join in a silly race,
While peas punch jokes with smiling grace.

Avocados flaunting their silly shades,
Cabbages rocking in floral parades,
Kiwi and lime make smoothies bright,
As the beets break into a funky night.

In this lush haven, laughter's the scheme,
Every fruit living their wildest dream,
With every giggle echoing clear,
Creating a hug for the heart to steer.

## **Island Whimsy**

In a land where coconuts chuckle,
And the sun winks with glee,
The fruit hangs in laughter,
Tickling the goofiness free.

Palm trees dance in the breeze,
With a topsy-turvy tune,
While laughter echoes like waves,
Beneath the silver moon.

Juicy jests drip from the sky,
Like confetti on a cake,
Mangoes play hopscotch with joy,
While bananas twist and shake.

In this quirky little paradise,
Every bite's a silly dare,
So grab a slice of folly,
And let your worries spare!

## Enchanted Orchard Wishes

In a grove of giggling fruits,
Where laughter seems to sprout,
Cherries wear tiny hats,
And oranges dance about.

The flowers gossip in the shade,
Telling tales of sweet delight,
As juicy secrets tumble down,
Inviting all to bite.

Beneath the apple's cheeky grin,
Dreams take flight and swirl,
Where plump pears play pranks on stars,
In a fruity, funny whirl.

Join the revelry of the brave,
In this orchard of surprise,
Where every slice brings chuckles,
And joy that never dies!

## **Serenity in a Golden Peel**

In the land of sunny giggles,
Where laughter peels like fruit,
Yellow slices of sunshine,
Make even the grumpiest hoot.

Gleeful fruits roll on the grass,
Juggling in a silly game,
While splashes of citrus splash smiles,
Turning serious to tame.

With whispers of playful breezes,
And breezy giggles in the air,
One bite of the golden cheer,
Casts away all care.

So wander through this garden bright,
Where joy is always near,
And find your heart in folly,
Let laughter lead the cheer!

## The Essence of Island Mirth


In a world of quirky flavors,
Where the bizarre fruit spills,
Bananas wear charming shoes,
While lemons trip on hills.

The island hums a silly tune,
Where coconuts hide laughs,
As grapes play tag with seagulls,
In fruity aftermaths.

Every bite sparks a chuckle,
Every sip, a giddy cheer,
In this land of joyous fruits,
Worries vanish like mist here.

So join the feast of laughter,
Let your heart be light and free,
In this realm of goofy flavors,
Where silliness makes thee!

## A Symphony of Flavors

In a land of yellow delight,
Fruits wear crowns, oh what a sight!
Glorious tangy sips align,
Take a bite, oh so divine!

Dancing with a hint of zest,
Tropical treats that never rest.
Laughter bubbles in each bite,
Mirthful munching, pure delight!

Gather 'round the juicy feast,
Imagination released.
Candied smiles on every face,
What a joy this fruity race!

Chasing taste on warm, bright days,
Serenity in silly ways.
With every crunch and goofy crunch,
Parading flavors in a bunch!

## Juicy Vistas

In the fields where sunlight beams,
Lemonade and laughter streams.
Golden globes that twist and sway,
Sun-kissed joys invite the play!

With a splash, a juicy shine,
Yummy quirks in each design.
Sipping sunshine's sweet embrace,
Running wild in this fresh space!

Giggles rise like breezy tides,
Through the laughter, joy abides.
Melon hats that fit just right,
Silly games that last all night!

Riding waves of fruity cheer,
Wondrous flavors drawing near.
Tropical whispers fill the skies,
In this land of tasty highs!

## Island Reveries

Underneath the swaying palms,
Laughter floats with fruity balms.
Tickles of a tangy breeze,
Tickling taste buds with such ease!

Blissful dances in the sun,
Every mouthful is such fun.
Mango hats and coconut shells,
Weaving tales that laughter tells!

Oh to dream on sandy shores,
Where fruity fantasies outpours.
Life's a bowl of sweet delight,
Bubbling joys that feel just right!

In the golden warmth we play,
Beneath the sun's bright, shining ray.
Giggling bites as friendships blend,
In this land where smiles can mend!

## The Golden Tides

Waves of laughter crash and gleam,
Fruity wonders crown the dream.
Sandy toes and silly quirks,
Joyful munching, blissful perks!

On the shores of tangy bliss,
Life is sweeter, can't resist!
Wobbling bowls of sun-kissed gold,
Stories of the fun unfold!

Rolling on the fruit parade,
Happy hearts in bright cascade.
Each sweet morsel brings a grin,
Splashing joy where dreams begin!

So come along, unleash your cheer,
In this land where all is clear.
Every bite a giggle high,
With laughter echoing the sky!

## Sunkissed Tranquility

Under the sun, we lounge and sway,
Wearing hats, bright as a summer day.
Lemonade spills, and laughter rings,
Joyful chaos, oh what fun it brings!

Flip-flops flip, the sand's so warm,
Dancing crabs create a swarm.
With fruity drinks, we laugh and cheer,
Life is sweet, come sip and steer!

Sunburnt noses, a rosy glow,
Belly-flops cause a splashy show.
In this paradise, we play and tease,
Time's a rabid dog, with no time to freeze!

Chasing seagulls, they steal our fries,
A feathery thief with mischievous eyes.
But what a thrill, to roam this space,
In sun-kissed bliss, we love this place!

## Honeyed Horizons

On sandy shores where laughter flies,
Goofy hats and silly ties.
Sunset drips like gooey gold,
While tales of clumsiness unfold.

A beach ball bounces, then pops with zest,
Turning friends into a silly quest.
With sticky fingers and ice cream smiles,
We waddle around in joyful styles!

Beneath the stars, we bring our snacks,
Laughter echoing, never lacks.
A dreamy night with quirky schemes,
All spinning in our honeyed dreams!

So raise your glass, let's toast tonight,
To funny stories, pure delight.
With every giggle, the joy expands,
In honeyed horizons, we take our stands!

## **Coral Dreams**

At dawn's first light, we frolic and run,
Chasing fish and having fun.
The ocean sings its bubbly song,
In coral dreams where we belong.

With beachcomber hats, we strut with flair,
On wobbly legs, we dance in air.
The tide pulls back with ocean's might,
With a splash, we laugh, what a silly sight!

Seashells whisper secrets so grand,
Tickling toes of each child and man.
With giggles rising, we jump and shout,
What life's about, we dance it out!

Bouncing on waves, we ride the foam,
Finding treasure, never alone.
In these coral dreams, forever stay,
With every chuckle, we savor the play!

## Resplendent Echoes

In a garden bright, where colors burst,
Flops and tumbles, the day's well cursed!
With chocolate drips and laughter loud,
We're silly souls, so blissfully proud.

Squeaky toys and playful squeals,
Tickling secrets and round-o'-wheels.
Each echo brightens the quiet air,
Spreading joy without a care!

With kooky dance moves, we take the stage,
With every slip, we turn the page.
Merriment blooms like daisies in spring,
Come join the laughter, oh what a fling!

Sunset wraps us in a warm embrace,
We flip our hair, enjoy the chase.
In resplendent echoes, we'll stay entwined,
In the garden of laughter, forever aligned!

## **Sun-Kissed Fantasies**

Beneath the sun's warm grin, so bright,
A fruit with spikes, a curious sight.
It wears a crown upon its head,
And dreams of beaches, where we tread.

With laughter ringing in the air,
We dance and prance without a care.
A tropical twist in every bite,
Juicy joy, a sheer delight.

Pick a slice, taste the zing,
It's like a happy summer fling.
With friends and fun, we share a laugh,
Chasing shadows on the grass.

So let the good times roll in heaps,
As silly thoughts and sweetness leaps.
In fruity realms, we dare to play,
Where every moment's a sunny day.

## The Essence of Summer Bliss

In gardens lush, a playful glee,
Fruit with armor, wild and free.
Sipping nectar, feeling bold,
A taste of sunshine, bright and gold.

With every bite, a giggle's near,
A squishy treat we hold so dear.
We brainstorm ways to cut it right,
Innocent laughter, pure delight.

As summer breezes kiss our skin,
We wear a smile, let joy begin.
Sun hats and shades, we find our groove,
With fruity puns, we all approve.

So gather 'round, the fruit is here,
Let's toast to joy and spread the cheer.
For every slice, a tale to weave,
In this sweet season, we believe.

## A Cascade of Citrus

A fruit parade, so bright and bold,
With stories waiting to be told.
In juicy rivers, laughter flows,
As we explore and joy bestows.

Let's slice and dice with giddy flair,
A fruity crown we all can wear.
Citrus zest, a worthier foe,
In cheeky games, we steal the show.

From dips to desserts, it finds its place,
In fruity fashion, we embrace.
Silly faces made with glee,
This fruity fun is wild and free.

With splashes bright, we laugh and sing,
In sunlit moments, let joy spring.
Join the fiesta, raise a cheer,
For fruity wonders, let's revere!

## **Fragrant Echoes of the Shore**

By the shore where sand meets spray,
A curious fruit joins in the play.
With beach balls flying high and free,
A tangy twist of jubilee.

In seagull squawks, our laughter rings,
As we discover what summer brings.
Flip-flops dancing, toes in sand,
Juicy treasures close at hand.

Waves crash in with a splish and splash,
Creamy treats that make us dash.
With tropical spins on every bite,
We feast on flavors, pure delight.

So let the sun set on our spree,
In citrus evenings, let's agree.
That every moment, sweet and true,
Is best enjoyed with friends like you.

## Tropic Skies

Under the tropic sun, we dance,
With fruity hats and a funny stance.
Waves tickle toes on golden sand,
As laughter spreads across the land.

Coconuts crack with a playful cheer,
While seagulls mock with a silly leer.
Banana peels slip on the way,
Turning quick steps to a comic display.

Hammocks sway in a gentle breeze,
Filled with giggles and just a tease.
While sunburns glow like a bright red wink,
We sip our drinks and start to stink.

Palm trees swaying, oh what a sight,
As we sing loud into the night.
With every joke that we cheerfully weave,
In this sunny space, who needs to leave?

## **Essence of Sunshine**

Bright as a fruit, oh what a twist,
In this sunny land, we can't resist.
Juicy laughter drips in the air,
As fruity follies lead us to dare.

Sunglasses on, we strut with flair,
Twirling in circles, without a care.
Lemonade spills, a slippery path,
As giggles echo, igniting our wrath.

With every sunset, a silly pose,
Making memories, the fun only grows.
Sun-kissed cheeks and a beaming grin,
In this sweet bliss, let the fun begin!

Rainbow hats capsize our delight,
As we race crabs in a whimsical fight.
All of life's flavor on this wild ride,
In this sunshine joy, we take great pride.

## Vibrant Reverberations

Bouncy rhythms fill the day,
With a touch of humor in every play.
Jokes on the beach, like sand in our hair,
As giggles bounce with no time to spare.

Swaying plants keep time with our song,
While mischief's laughter can't be wrong.
Citrus smiles shine bright and bold,
As wacky tales just have to be told.

Kites fly high in the clear blue sky,
Each twist and turn, we can't help but cry.
With snacks galore that we share around,
In this vibrant chaos, true joy is found.

Swinging on vines like Tarzan's crew,
Making a mess, it's what we do.
Under the sun, let the good times roll,
With happy hearts, we take a stroll.

## **Tropical Echoes**

Echoes of laughter bounce in the sea,
As waves giggle back, wild and free.
Bright colors splash all over the place,
In this nonsensical, joyful race.

Mango mischief in the air,
Silly antics everywhere!
We toss our drinks in a playful fight,
As the sun dips low, painting the night.

Shells make music, a random beat,
While dancing crabs tap their tiny feet.
With a wink and a nudge, let's share a toast,
To the quirkiest moments we love the most!

By evening's glow, the giggles blend,
Creating memories that never end.
In this tropical land of silly schemes,
We find our joy in the wildest dreams.

## **The Allure of Bliss**

In a world where laughter spins,
A wobbly fruit with prickly fins.
Its crown stands tall, a regal sight,
Awakens giggles, pure delight.

Juicy bites, a sugary cheer,
Dancing in the summer air.
We wear our hats made of sweet slice,
And savor every juicy vice.

Oh, sweet nectar, a funny prank,
Falling off our fruit-stacked bank.
Who knew bliss could be this bright?
In each yellow bite, pure light.

Poolside toss in a sunny fling,
Sipping juice while the parrots sing.
This golden globe of all things fun,
Brings on a joy that weighs a ton.

## Tangles of Sunshine

There's a twist in every slice I see,
As goofy glee surrounds the spree.
A fruit that wears such sassy skins,
   It even giggles when it spins!

With zesty bursts, the taste parade,
   Every bite, a sweet charade.
Sunshine dances on my tongue,
And merry tunes are always sung.

A crown of points, a zest for fun,
Who knew snacks could become such puns?
We toss it high, it lands with flair,
   In this comedy, we all share!

Laughter bubbles, the day's delight,
In a world so silly, where smiles ignite.
Roll out the quirks, let joy collide,
In tangles of sunshine, we all abide.

## Fragrant Daydreams

In gardens where the laughter blooms,
A fruity bomb, it brightly looms.
A fragrant dance, a silly spin,
Every nibble brings a grin!

With punchy hues and a laugh or two,
This fruit turns gray skies into blue.
Wiggly bits, a delightful heap,
That tickles our taste buds from deep.

Adventures in every tiny bite,
Like a cheerful hug, oh, what a sight!
I toss my cares to gold-streaked air,
In fragrant daydreams, laughter's fair.

So gather 'round, share the zest,
In the fruity fest, we're truly blessed.
A party of giggles, all the way,
This aroma turns dull into play!

## A Tidal Wave of Joy

A wave of sweetness crashes in,
With tangy waves that make us grin.
In a fruit that jests with every chew,
   We surf the flavors, me and you.

Salty breeze mixed with juicy cheer,
  Like jellyfish that laugh and sneer.
Tasting sunshine with every dip,
  We ride the tides on a juicy trip.

Flip-flops clatter, giggling loud,
As we feast beneath a sunny cloud.
In sticky hands, the joy flows free,
This tidal wave, just you and me!

So let the laughter splash around,
With a fruity joy that knows no bounds.
  A tidal wave, a fruity spree,
   In this adventure, we all agree!

## **Delightful Tropics**

In the land where sunbeams dance,
Fruits wear their silly pants.
Coconuts laugh at tall piñatas,
While monkeys play their funny guitars.

Limes jump into coconut pools,
Bananas act like silly fools.
With bright umbrellas sipping shade,
These juicy antics never fade.

Bikini-clad fruits wave hello,
In a fruit parade down below.
Watermelons glide with glee,
While papayas sing in harmony.

Here in bliss, who needs a scheme?
Life's a riot, a juicy dream!
Just laugh and sway under the trees,
As nature plays its funny tease.

## Radiant Expectations

In the tropics, the sun takes a bow,
With fruity faces laughing, wow!
Mangoes waltz on sandy floors,
While guavas tell the best of stories.

A coconut spins in a grassy twirl,
While papaya blushes, oh what a whirl!
Bananas slip on the bright blue slide,
Joy bursts forth, can't be denied.

Orange slices cheer as they roll,
Chasing limes that take a stroll.
The rhythm of sweet, zesty fun,
In this paradise, laughs are never done!

With each wave of the ocean's flow,
Fruits giggle under the sun's glow.
Basking in this fruity jam,
Life here's a wild candy slam!

## The Taste of Paradise

Beneath the trees, the fruits conspire,
Creating flavors that never tire.
Pineapple hats and citrus laughs,
In the sun, they dance on their wafts.

Papaya plays peekaboo with the sun,
While mangoes roll, having too much fun.
A whole brigade of fruity pals,
Chasing jellyfish in colorful thralls.

Bananas slip and slide on the shore,
Toasting with cherries and asking for more.
Lively nor orange, what a feast,
With the ocean waves as their playful beast!

Dreams burst forth with every bite,
In this realm, everything feels so right.
Dive into laughter, the sweetest spree,
For here, every day is a jubilee!

## Sun-Kissed Wishes

Under the beams, the fruits collide,
Spinning tales with joyful pride.
Kiwis wear their sunglasses cool,
While guavas jump in the bubbly pool.

Strawberries giggle, bursting with cheer,
Tropics are the laugh we hold dear.
Pineapple hats upon their crowns,
Fruit kingdoms in our comical towns.

Lemons toss confetti in the air,
While melons roll round without a care.
Life is a carnival of zest,
In sun-splashed lands, we feel blessed.

With every sip of the fruity breeze,
We find joy in the silliest tease.
In this tangled web of golden light,
Sun-kissed wishes dance into the night.

## Whimsical Harvests

In fields of yellow, fruit shall grow,
A crown of spikes, a sunny show,
Wearing shades, they dance in glee,
A fruity party, just for me.

With every slice, a laughter loud,
They gather 'round, a merry crowd,
With silly hats and goofy grins,
In juicy joy, the fun begins.

The sound of laughter fills the air,
As fruit parade without a care,
They twirl and spin, what a delight,
A zesty dream that feels just right.

So join the feast, let's make a toast,
To weird delights we love the most,
In every bite, there's joy to share,
A harvest of laughter everywhere.

## Fruits of Fantasy

In orchards where the colors blend,
The fruits are talking, what a trend,
With wild ideas, they dream awake,
A juicy tale they love to make.

Bananas wearing capes of green,
Coconut kings, so proud, they're mean,
Mandarins play hide and seek,
While berries giggle, cheek to cheek.

They tell of adventures in the sun,
Of pirate ships and racing fun,
With every crunch, a secret spills,
The laughter grows, it surely thrills.

So gather round, enjoy the scene,
With every bite, you'll feel serene,
A fruity world of jest and cheer,
In vibrant colors, bring us near.

## Solstice Celebrations

As sunbeams dance on juicy crowns,
Fruits in hats parade through towns,
With laughter loud and spirits bright,
They celebrate from day to night.

Watermelon slides down the hill,
Pineapple troops with vibes to thrill,
In a carnival of silly games,
Their quirkiest smiles bring them fame.

Tropical tunes fill up the air,
Kiwi clowns perform without a care,
With every bite, a carnival cheer,
The joyous fruits draw everyone near.

So let us dance, let spirits soar,
In jolly feasts, we crave for more,
With fruity friends all 'round the floor,
A festival of laughs galore.

# **Dreamy Tropics**

In lands where coconuts take flight,
And mangoes twirl like stars at night,
They tell of dreams in fruity rhyme,
Where silliness meets summer time.

They lounge on beaches made of zest,
In sunny hats, they look their best,
Juggling flavors, a splash of fun,
Each fruity star beneath the sun.

With piña coladas on their mind,
They laugh aloud, so sweet and kind,
In every sip, a whisper shared,
A fantasy where no one's scared.

So join the dream, let laughter flow,
In this tropical show, you'll glow,
With every slice, the fun will burst,
In dreamy lands, we quench our thirst.

www.ingramcontent.com/pod-product-compliance
Lightning Source LLC
Chambersburg PA
CBHW070304120526
44590CB00017B/2554